Cambridge Direct Mathematics

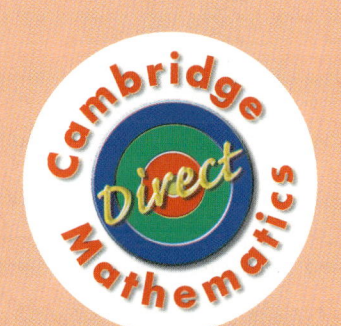

Calculations

4

CAMBRIDGE UNIVERSITY PRESS

PUBLISHED BY THE PRESS SYNDICATE OF THE UNIVERSITY OF CAMBRIDGE
The Pitt Building, Trumpington Street, Cambridge, United Kingdom

CAMBRIDGE UNIVERSITY PRESS
The Edinburgh Building, Cambridge CB2 2RU, UK
40 West 20th Street, New York, NY 10011–4211, USA
10 Stamford Road, Oakleigh, VIC 3166, Australia
Ruiz de Alarcón 13, 28014 Madrid, Spain
Dock House, The Waterfront, Cape Town 8001, South Africa

http://www.cambridge.org

© Cambridge University Press 2000

First published 2000

Printed in the United Kingdom at the University Press, Cambridge

Typefaces Frutiger, Helvetica, Minion, Swift *System* QuarkXPress 4.03®

A catalogue record for this book is available from the British Library

ISBN 0 521 78470 0 paperback

Text illustration by Adam Stower

General editors for Cambridge Mathematics Direct
Sandy Cowling, Jane Crowden, Andrew King, Jeanette Mumford

Writing team for *Calculations 4*
Anne Barber, Lynn Huggins-Cooper, Sandy Cowling, Zubeida Dasgupta, Gill Hatch, Gary Murrell, Marian Reynolds, Fay Turner

The writers and publishers would like to thank the many schools and individuals
who trialled lessons for Cambridge Mathematics Direct.

NOTICE TO TEACHERS
It is illegal to reproduce any part of this work in material form (including photocopying and electronic storage)
except under the following circumstances:
(i) where you are abiding by a licence granted to your school or institution by the Copyright Licensing Agency;
(ii) where no such licence exists, or where you wish to exceed the terms of a licence, and you have
gained the written permission of Cambridge University Press;
(iii) where you are allowed to reproduce without permission under the provisions of Chapter 3 of
the Copyright, Designs and Patents Act 1988.

Abbreviations and symbols
IP Interactive picture
CM Copymaster
A is practice work
B develops ideas
C is extension work
★ if needed, helps with work in A
A red margin indicates that children work with the teacher.
A green margin indicates that children work independently.

Contents

Addition and subtraction (AS)

AS1	**Understanding addition and subtraction**	
AS1.3	Subtraction as taking away	6
AS1.4	Solving problems	8
AS1.5	Checking subtraction by adding	10

AS2	**Using significant digits to add: from mental to informal written methods**	
AS2.1	Explaining how to add	12
AS2.2	Splitting numbers to add	14
AS2.4	Recording addition of several numbers	16
AS2.5	Adding money in columns	18

AS3	**Adjusting and compensating: from mental to informal written methods**	
AS3.2	Adding and adjusting	21
AS3.3	Subtracting and adjusting	22
AS3.4	Add too much and take away	24
AS3.5	Solving addition problems	26

AS4	**Extending mental strategies: developing a standard written method**	
AS4.1	Halving and doubling	28
AS4.3	Doubling 10s	29
AS4.4	Using different strategies to add and subtract	31
AS4.5	Choosing ways to add in columns	32

AS5	**Developing strategies for 3- and 4-digit numbers: mental and informal written methods**	
AS5.1	Using pattern to add a single digit	33
AS5.2	Using pattern to subtract a single digit 1	34
AS5.3	Using pattern to subtract a single digit 2	36
AS5.5	Using addition and subtraction facts	37

AS6	**Subtraction by counting up**	
AS6.3	Reaching the next hundred	39
AS6.5	HTU – HTU: Subtraction by counting up	42

AS7	**Adding with carrying**	
AS7.1	Starting with the units	44
AS7.2	A short way of recording in columns	46
AS7.3	Carrying to other columns	47
AS7.5	Adding several numbers in columns	48

AS8	**Subtraction with decomposition**	
AS8.2	Adjusting from tens to units to help subtract	49
AS8.4	Subtracting 3-digit numbers	50

Multiplication and division (MD)

MD1	**Understanding multiplication and division**	
MD1.1	Add and multiply	51
MD1.3	Multiply and divide	53

MD2	**Using known multiplication facts**	
MD2.2	Which way round?	55
MD2.4	Using multiplication facts 1	56

MD3	**Using the associative and distributive laws for TU × U**	
MD3.1	Using multiplication facts 2	58
MD3.2	Multiplying with money	59

MD4	**Developing informal written methods for TU ÷ U**	
MD4.1	Sharing equally	60
MD4.2	Rounding	61
MD4.4	Dividing bigger numbers	63

MD5	**Working towards short multiplication for TU × U**	
MD5.1	Multiplying by 10 or 100	64
MD5.2	Multiplying by 'near 10' numbers	66

MD6	**More ways to multiply TU × U: short multiplication**	
MD6.1	Multiplying quickly	68
MD6.2	Using columns for TU × U	69
MD6.3	TU × U: tens first	71
MD6.4	TU × U: units first	72
MD6.5	TU × U: short multiplication	73
MD7	**Towards a standard form for TU ÷ U**	
MD7.2	Dividing 2-digit numbers	74
MD7.3	Using columns to record TU ÷ U	76
MD7.4	Introducing short division	78

Solving problems (SP)

SP1	**Solving problems 1**	
SP1.2	Patterns and rules	80
SP1.3	Finding solutions	82
SP1.4	Explaining word problems	84
SP2	**Solving problems 2**	
SP2.2	Explaining how to ...	85
SP3	**Solving problems 3**	
SP3.1	Using + and − to solve problems	87
SP3.2	Choosing which way to add or subtract	89
SP3.3	Using × and ÷ to solve problems	90
SP3.5	Solving multi-step problems	92

AS1.3 Subtraction as taking away

> **Key idea** 500 − 300 is not the same as 300 − 500.

A1 How much has been used?
Write a number sentence for each one.

	a	b	c	d	e	f	g
Stock	White paint	Black pens	Bulldog clips	Erasers	Red markers	Chalk	Pencils
Quantity in January	70 tubs	400	400	500	80	1200 sticks	1500
Quantity in April	30 tubs	150	260	220	40	700 sticks	800

B1 Look at the amount of stock in April in the chart in A1.

- **a** Miss Bennett's class took 20 tubs of white paint. How many are left now?

- **b** Sarah dropped and broke 300 sticks of chalk.
  How many whole sticks are left?

- **c** 30 of the black pens do not work.
  How many do work?

- **d** Class 3 did a lot of drawing and needed 30 erasers.
  How many are left now?

6 AS1 Understanding addition and subtraction

B2

	a	b	c	d
	White paper	Sugar paper	Tracing paper	Cartridge paper
Number of sheets in September	9500	8200	5000	6700
Number of sheets in October	8300	7600	4100	5400

Write number sentences to show how much has been used.

C1 The chart in A1 shows how much stock was left at the end of one term.

Will there be enough stock for the next term?

If not, how much more is needed?

C2 The chart in B2 shows how much paper was used in one month.

How many more months will each type of paper last for?

Key idea | 500 − 300 is not the same as 300 − 500.

AS1 Understanding addition and subtraction

AS1.4 Solving problems

> **Key idea** We can use all the things we know about numbers to solve problems mentally.

★1 You need place value cards.

a 23 + 10 = ☐   b 69 + 10 = ☐

c 120 + 10 = ☐   d 135 + 10 = ☐

Change the tens digit only.

★2 a 26 + 20 = ☐   b 49 + 30 = ☐

c 120 + 20 = ☐   d 120 + 30 = ☐

A1 a 342 + 10 = ☐   b 342 + 20 = ☐   c 342 + 30 = ☐

A2 a 225 + ☐ = 245   b 125 + ☐ = 175   c 308 + ☐ = 338

A3 Baythorp Junior School has 196 children.

Mrs Staple needs to order exercise books for the new school year.

This is what is left at the end of the term.

Exercise books
a blue   146
b red   108
c yellow   134
d green   103

The books come in packs of 10.

Each child needs one of each colour.

How many packs must Mrs Staple order?

Write a number sentence for a – d

B1 Mrs Staple needs to order writing equipment for 196 children at Baythorp Junior School.

All the items come in packs of 10.

The table shows you what the children need.

It also shows what is in the stock cupboard.

		Children need	How many in the stock cupboard
a	Rulers	1 each	106
b	Pencils	2 each	310
c	Pens	4 each	702
d	Erasers	1 between 2	53
e	Pencil sharpeners	1 between 4	36

How many packs must Mrs Staple order?

Write a number sentence for **a** – **e**

Remember that items come in 10s, and that 196 is nearly 200.

C1 You need to use IP 10.

Choose items to order. Make a stock list.

Find out how many of each item is needed.

Record your working clearly.

Items do not always come in 10s. You can decide.

| Key idea | We can use all the things we know about numbers to solve problems mentally. |

AS1 Understanding addition and subtraction

AS1.5 Checking subtraction by adding

> **Key idea**: We can check subtraction answers by adding: 265 − 20 = 245 is true because 245 + 20 = 265.

A1 How much money does each child have left?

a) Carrie had 76p and spent 30p

b) Lola had 54p and spent 40p

c) Sinda had 97p and spent 50p

A2 This is the school lunch register for the week.
Has Mr Kitchen worked out how many children had packed lunches correctly?

	a Monday	b Tuesday	c Wednesday	d Thursday	e Friday
Children at school	96	88	93	81	94
School dinner	30	40	40	40	50
Packed lunches	45	48	63	39	44

AS1 Understanding addition and subtraction

B1 Mark has a special numbers magic trick.
He picks cards from 3 piles and they should make a correct number sentence.
But it doesn't always work! Which answers are wrong?
What should the answers be?

a) 345 − 40 = 296

b) 793 − 60 = 719

c) 458 − 40 = 428

d) 861 − 50 = 801

e) 632 − 20 = 612

Key idea We can check subtraction answers by adding: 265 − 245 is true because 245 + 20 = 265.

AS1 Understanding addition and subtraction

AS2.1 Explaining how to add

> **Key idea** We can explain how we add numbers mentally by writing down each step.

A1 Find these totals.
Use number sentences to explain what you did.

a 60p + 24p = £ ☐
b 90p + 13p = £ ☐
c 70p + 29p = £ ☐
d 80p + 34p = £ ☐
e 50p + 48p = £ ☐

B1 Find these totals.
Use number sentences to explain what you did.

a £1.10 + 38p = £ ☐
b £1.50 + £1.23 = £ ☐
c 90p + 86p = £ ☐
d £3.80 + £1.62 = £ ☐

B2 Explain in writing how to work out these questions.

How many people went on the dodgems on

a Monday and Saturday?
b Tuesday and Wednesday?
c Friday and Sunday?
d Wednesday and Thursday?
e Friday and Saturday?

Number of people who went on the dodgems

Monday	250
Tuesday	399
Wednesday	580
Thursday	401
Friday	1430
Saturday	312
Sunday	263

AS2 Using significant digits to add: from mental to informal written methods

C1 Work out the missing numbers.

Explain your method in writing.

Number of people who went on the big wheel each day

	Morning	Afternoon	Total
Monday	250	145	☐
Tuesday	☐	223	543
Wednesday	1200	☐	1311
Thursday	470	225	☐
Friday	☐	641	851

C2

Hot dogs	£3.10
Burgers	£2.20
Fries	£1.70
Chicken nuggets	£2.50

Mints	44p
Sweets	55p
Candy floss	72p
Chews	23p

a If Ahmed buys a burger and candy floss, how much change will he get from a £5 note?

b Write number sentences to explain how you did **a**

c Investigate what you can buy for £10.

Key idea We can explain how we add numbers mentally by writing down each step.

AS2 Using significant digits to add: from mental to informal written methods

AS2.2 Splitting numbers to add

> **Key idea** We can split numbers into hundreds, tens and ones to add them mentally.

A1 Split these numbers into hundreds, tens and ones to help you add them together.

a 43 + 24 = ☐   b 28 + 51 = ☐

c 123 + 46 = ☐   d 64 + 203 = ☐

A2 a Write these prices in pence.

Teddy £4.20 / 420p
Duck £3.51 / p
Cowboy hat £1.33 / p
Monkey £2.01 / p
Frisbee £3.42 / p

b How much does it cost to buy

- a teddy and a duck?
- a cowboy hat and a teddy?
- a frisbee and a monkey?

B1 You have a £10 note to spend at the toy stall.

a Choose 2 or 3 things to buy.

b Work out the total cost. Make sure it is less than £10.

c Write a number sentence.

d Do **a** – **c** three more times.

AS2 Using significant digits to add: from mental to informal written methods

Some of the lucky dip numbers got blown out of the tub.
Lucy found them on the ground.

Take 2 tickets PRIZES for a total of 567

243   168   156   324   411

C1 **a** Find all the totals for 2 tickets.
There are 10.

b Which pairs win a prize?

C2 **a** Find all the totals for 3 tickets.

b Can you make the prize-winning total?

Record carefully.
Don't miss any totals.

Key idea | We can split numbers into hundreds, tens and ones to add them mentally.

AS2 Using significant digits to add: from mental to informal written methods

AS2.4 Recording addition of several numbers

Key idea | When we record in columns, units line up under units, tens under tens, and hundreds under hundreds.

A1 Add these numbers.

a) 1 6 6
  +   3 2

b) 3 4 3
  +   5 4

c) 4 3 1
  +   5 4

A2 These magic numbers win prizes

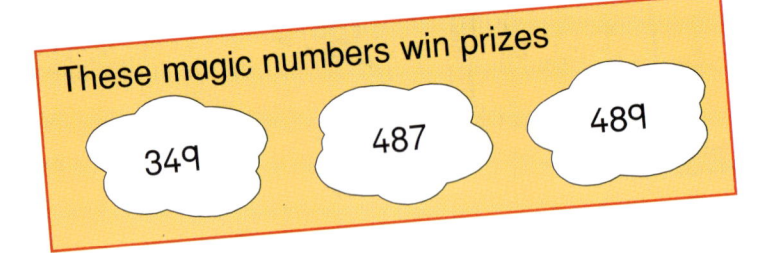

349   487   489

Set out your sums clearly. Start with the hundreds

5 children have bought magic number tickets.

Add up the numbers on each ticket to see who wins a prize.

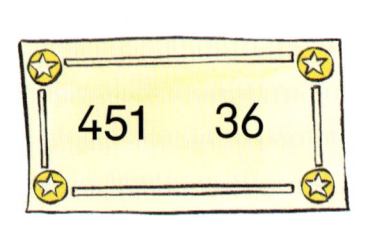

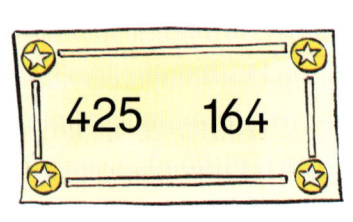

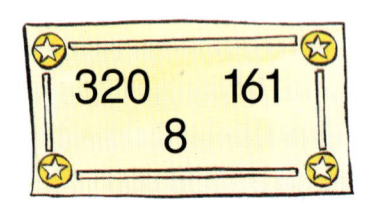

a) 451   36 — Gabriel

b) 307   12   30 — Lenny

c) 425   164 — Elizabeth

d) 403   96 — Jon

e) 320   161   8 — Emma

B1 People can buy tickets for the big wheel at the ride or at the entrance gate.

Mrs T. Icket recorded how many tickets were sold each hour.

	Big wheel	Gate
6 pm	156	35
7 pm	223	84
8 pm	95	128
9 pm	306	58

How many tickets were sold at

a 6 pm?   b 7 pm?   c 8 pm?   d 9 pm?

Record in columns

B2 a 481   b 357   c 864

Hit each coconut!
Find two 3-digit numbers that add to give its number.

C1 Hit the Coconut! 3 goes to Winning totals...

a 120   b 389   c 953

Find 3 numbers to add and hit a coconut.

Use these digits once only for each coconut.

0 1 2 3 4 5 6 7 8 9

Key idea When we record in columns, units line up under units, tens under tens, and hundreds under hundreds.

AS2 Using significant digits to add: from mental to informal written methods

AS2.5 Adding money in columns

> **Key idea** We can record in columns when we add amounts of money.

★1 Write the prices as pence.

a £1.37 b £3.02 c £0.99 d £2.98

★2 Write the prices as pounds and pence.

a 103p b 231p c 399p d 32p

A1 Add these prices together.

a £ 1.46
 + £ 3.11

b £ 2.13
 + £ 1.04

c £ 3.28
 + £ 1.37

d £ 2.01
   £ 2.13
 + £ 1.65

e £ 0.44
   £ 1.12
 + £ 2.03

f £ 5.63
   £ 3.21
 + £ 1.15

A2 How much does it cost to go on the

a big dipper and dodgems?

b helter skelter and dodgems?

c big dipper, ghost train and dodgems?

d helter skelter, tea cups and ghost train?

Ride prices
Big dipper £1.02
Helter skelter £1.33
Ghost train £1.67
Dodgems £1.29
Tea cups 68p

AS2 Using significant digits to add: from mental to informal written methods

B1 Mr Johnson recorded how much money he took at the weekend for the big dipper and for the helter skelter.

	Saturday	Sunday
Big dipper	£439	£543
Helter skelter	£215	£366

a How much did Mr Johnson take for the big dipper over the whole weekend?

b How much did he take altogether for the helter skelter on Saturday and Sunday?

c How much money did Mr Johnson take on Saturday?

B2

Gabriel £2.26
Elizabeth £4.03
Lenny £3.15
Jon £5.38
Emma £3.29

a How much money do Gabriel and Lenny have to spend altogether?

b How much money do Elizabeth and Jon have in total?

c What is the total value of the money in Emma and Lenny's purses?

d How much money do Gabriel, Lenny and Elizabeth have in total?

AS2 Using significant digits to add: from mental to informal written methods

C1 The hot dog seller printed out his till receipts at the end of the day.

He spilt ketchup over the receipts and cannot read some of the numbers.

a)
```
  £ 4.38
+ £ 2.25
  £ 6.00
  £ 0.🟥
+ £ 0.13
  £🟥.🟥
```

b)
```
  £ 2.57
+ £ 4.35
  £🟥.🟥
  £ 0.80
+ £🟥.🟥
  £🟥.🟥
```

c)
```
  £ 3.42
+ £ 5.39
  £ 1.10
  £🟥.🟥
  £🟥.🟥
+ £🟥.🟥
  £🟥.🟥
```

d)
```
  £🟥.32
+ £ 2.2🟥
  £ 3.🟥4
  £ 6.00
  £ 0.90
+ £ 0.15
  £🟥.🟥
```

C2 Work out the total of these prices.

a)
```
  £ 4.49
  £ 2.15
+ £ 1.36
```

b)
```
  £ 3.14
  £ 5.29
+ £ 1.65
```

c)
```
  £ 5.30
  £13.09
+ £ 2.63
```

d)
```
  £ 2.66
  £ 0.07
+ £ 3.99
```

Key idea We can record in columns when we add amounts of money.

AS2 Using significant digits to add: from mental to informal written methods

AS3.2 Adding and adjusting

> **Key idea**
> To add 9, 19, 29, . . ., add 10, 20, 30, . . . and subtract 1.
> To add 11, 21, 31, . . ., add 10, 20, 30, . . . and add 1.

B1 Use the adding and adjusting method to find the answer to these.

a) 38 + 29 = ☐
b) 164 + 31 = ☐
c) 73 + 59 = ☐
d) 291 + 21 = ☐
e) 245 + 99 = ☐
f) 159 + 41 = ☐

B2 Ravi has £1. He wants to buy a drink that costs 49p.
Which of these can he afford to buy as well?

a) Crisps 56p
b) Chocomints 24p
c) Orange blister 43p
d) Galloping gumballs 19p
e) Peppermints Pyramids 51p
f) Teatime trios 73p

C1 Ravi's friend has £2. She buys a lolly instead of a drink. The lolly costs 95p.
Which of the treats can she afford to buy as well?

C2 Choose treats for your friends. Don't spend more than £3.

AS3 Adjusting and compensating: from mental methods to informal written methods

AS3.3 Subtracting and adjusting

Key idea
To subtract 9, 19, 29, ..., subtract 10, 20, 30, ... and add 1.
To subtract 11, 21, 31, ..., subtract 10, 20, 30, ... and then subtract 1.

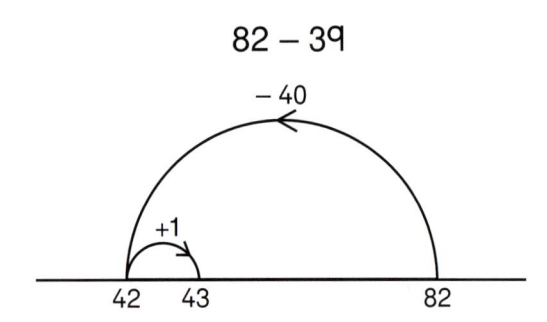

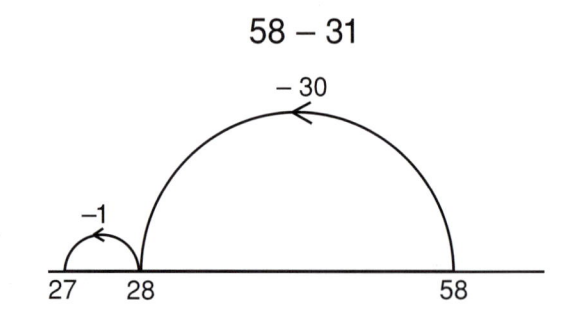

82 − 39

− 40
+1
42 43   82

58 − 31

− 30
−1
27 28   58

A1 Draw a number line to show your working.

a 67 − 19 = ☐   b 48 − 21 = ☐

c 53 − 31 = ☐   d 172 − 49 = ☐

A2 a Copy and complete this table.

Starting number	− 39	− 40	− 41
76			
92			
58			
84			

b Choose a row.
What do you notice about the numbers in it?

AS3 Adjusting and compensating: from mental methods to informal written methods

B1 In the sale all these things are 49p cheaper.
How much does each cost?

B2 What if ...?
Each item is 61p cheaper instead.
How much does each cost?

You cannot use multiples of 10.

C1 Find 4 pairs of numbers with a difference of 29.

C2 Find 4 pairs of numbers with a difference of 41.

C3 Choose 1 of the numbers below.
Find 3 pairs of numbers with that difference.

Use numbers with 2 or 3 digits, or even 4 or more!

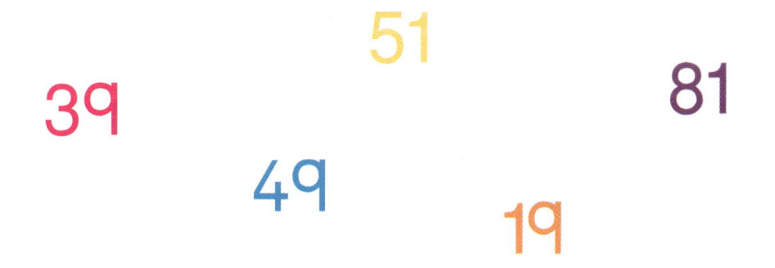

39   51   49   19   81

| Key idea | To subtract 9, 19, 29, . . ., subtract 10, 20, 30, . . . and add 1.
To subtract 11, 21, 31, . . ., subtract 10, 20, 30, . . . and then subtract 1. |

AS3 Adjusting and compensating: from mental methods to informal written methods

AS3.4 Add too much and take away

> **Key idea** Sometimes it is easier to add too much and then take off.

138 + 95 = 233

```
  138
+ 100
  238
-   5
  233
```

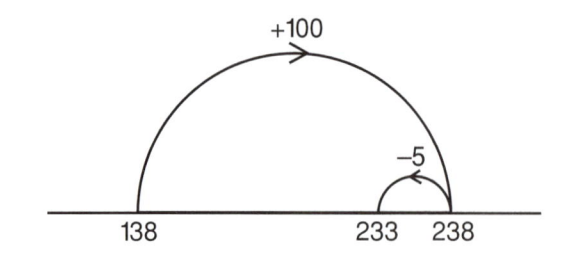

Add too much but choose an easy number!

A1 Show your working on a number line.

a 168 + 97 = ☐   b 329 + 68 = ☐

c 226 + 94 = ☐   d 184 + 48 = ☐

A2 Penny and James enjoy looking at minibeasts.

They measure how far each one travelled in $\frac{1}{2}$ minute and then in another 2 minutes.

	millipede	ant	caterpillar	snail
$\frac{1}{2}$ minute	88 cm	94 cm	19 cm	8 cm
2 minutes	284 cm	379 cm	83 cm	29 cm

What is the total distance each minibeast travelled in $2\frac{1}{2}$ minutes?

AS3 Adjusting and compensating: from mental methods to informal written methods

Set 1: 275, 154, 426, 268, 347

Set 2: 75, 94, 69, 195, 37

B1 Pick a card from each set.
Add the numbers together.

B2 Do B1 four more times.
Use each card once.

C1 Look at the minibeasts in A2.

How far did these pairs travel in 2 minutes?
Show your working.

a millipede and snail

b millipede and caterpillar

c ant and caterpillar

d millipede and ant

C2 Compare your working for C1 with a friend's.

Discuss all the strategies you could have used.

Decide which is best for each sum, ready for the plenary.

| Key idea | Sometimes it is easier to add too much and then take off. |

AS3 Adjusting and compensating: from mental methods to informal written methods

AS3.5 Solving addition problems

> **Key idea** Sometimes it is easy to use an 'adjusting' strategy to solve addition problems.

Children in class 4 are planning a display of pictures for the hall.

They are making pictures with dried beans, lentils and pasta.

In the stock cupboard are partly used packets.

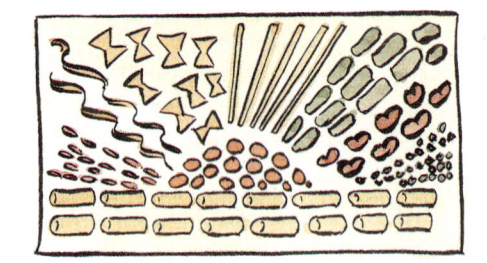

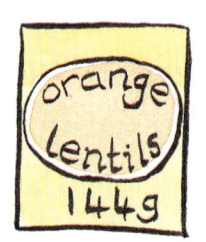

Packets shown:
- red beans 217g
- orange lentils 144g
- yellow beans 274g
- black lentils 127g
- red beans 79g
- yellow beans 93g
- pasta shapes 123g
- black lentils 122g
- pasta shapes 179g
- orange lentils 108g

Show your working for each question.

B1 Find out the total weight of

  a red beans   **b** yellow beans   **c** orange lentils

B2 **a** 2 children each need 150 g of pasta.
Is there enough pasta?

  b 10 children need 25 g of black lentils each.
Are there enough lentils?

This is the plan for the display.

(Display plan: 100 cm tall × 200 cm wide, with pictures by Joe, Abigail, Max, Sean, Fiona, Oliver, Sita, Ruth, Ravi, Tanya — "Sunsets by class 4")

The children can use up these materials from the stock cupboard.

Stock list	Length	Length	Length
backing paper (100 cm wide)	45 cm	109 cm	46 cm
border paper	306 cm	137 cm	148 cm
card for names	74 cm	89 cm	137 cm

C1 Find out if there is enough

   a backing paper   **b** border paper

Show your working.

C2 Each picture has a name card 25 cm long.
Is there enough card?
Show your working.

C3 Discuss the methods you used with a partner.
Decide who had the best method for each question.
Be ready to explain why in the plenary.

Key idea Sometimes it is easy to use an 'adjusting' strategy to solve addition problems.

AS3 Adjusting and compensating: from mental methods to informal written methods

AS4.1 Halving and doubling

Key idea	We can check halving by doubling.

B1 Half shares

Classes 4H and 4R share the coloured pencils that are left in the boxes.

Each class takes half of every colour.

Check that their calculations are fair.

Record your working.

You can do it by doubling.

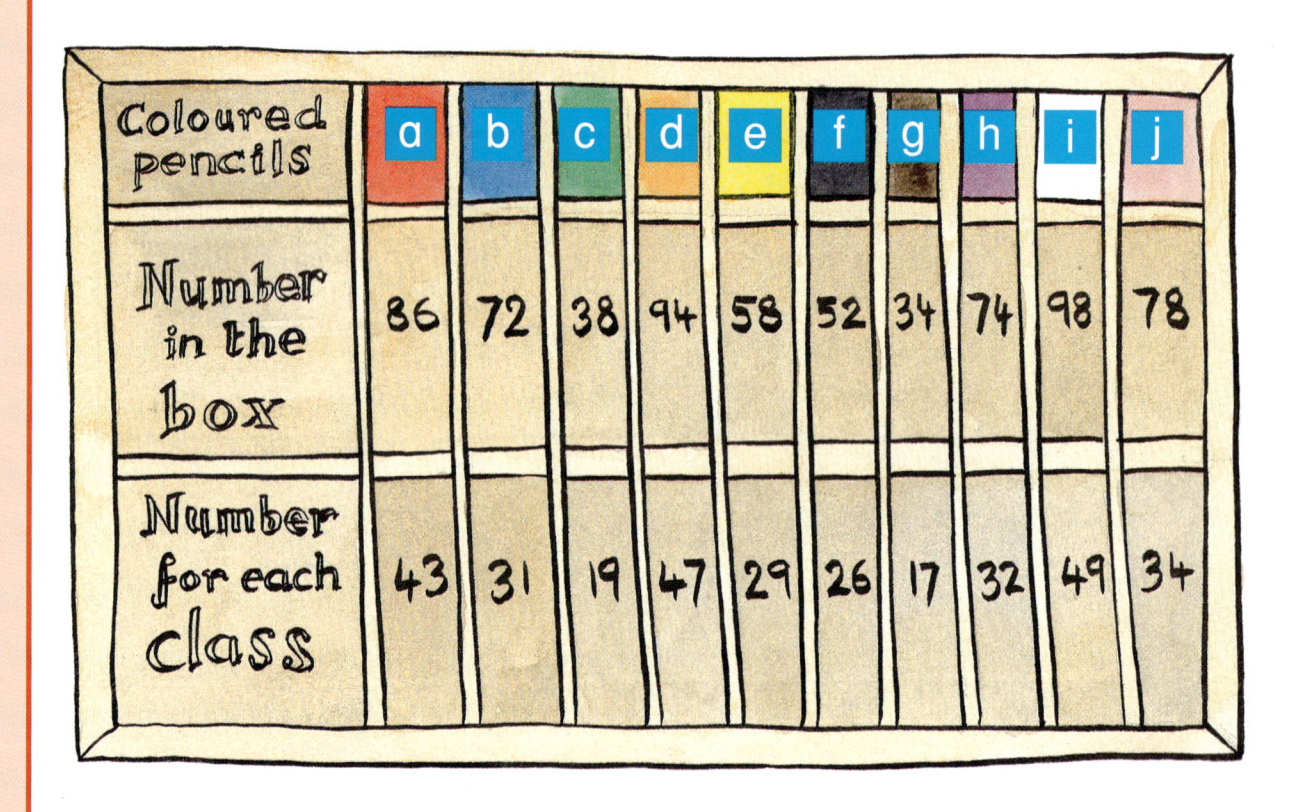

Coloured pencils	a	b	c	d	e	f	g	h	i	j
Number in the box	86	72	38	94	58	52	34	74	98	78
Number for each class	43	31	19	47	29	26	17	32	49	34

C1 You need IP 5.

Make up some doubling or halving problems to swap with a partner.

Swap back and check their answers by halving or doubling.

AS4.3 Doubling 10s

| Key idea | We can use doubles of multiples of 10 to check calculations using measures. |

★1 Double these.

a 40   b 200   c 90   d 500

Remember doubling 20 is the same as (double 2) × 10

★2 a About how long are 2 skipping ropes? (139 cm)

b About how long are 2 tables? (209 cm)

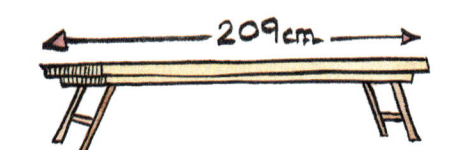

A1 Double these.

a 80   b 130   c 250   d 410
e 360   f 190   g 350   h 470

A2 Alastair needs to make a menu for the refreshment stall at the school fair.

His piece of card is 60 cm wide.

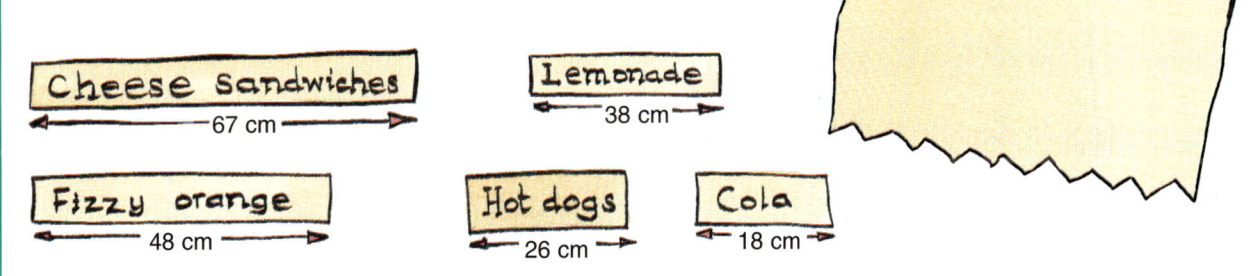

Cheese sandwiches — 67 cm
Lemonade — 38 cm
Fizzy orange — 48 cm
Hot dogs — 26 cm
Cola — 18 cm

He has made some labels for the menu.

a Which ones will fit and which ones will not?

b Can he put HOT DOGS and FIZZY ORANGE on the same line?

Work out which labels he can fit on the same line.

Check your answers by rounding the measurements to the nearest 10.

AS4 Extending mental strategies: developing a standard written method

B1 Each banner needs two strips of paper, one for the front and one for the back.

About how much paper do you need for each banner?

a 211 cm RIDE-A-DONKEY

b 158 cm Hamburgers

c 127 cm Coconut shy

d 277 cm Roll-a-Penny Stall

e 386 cm School Summer Fair

f 492 cm SATURDAY 10th JUNE at 1 PM

C1 Cassy's mum has bought a new shelf unit.

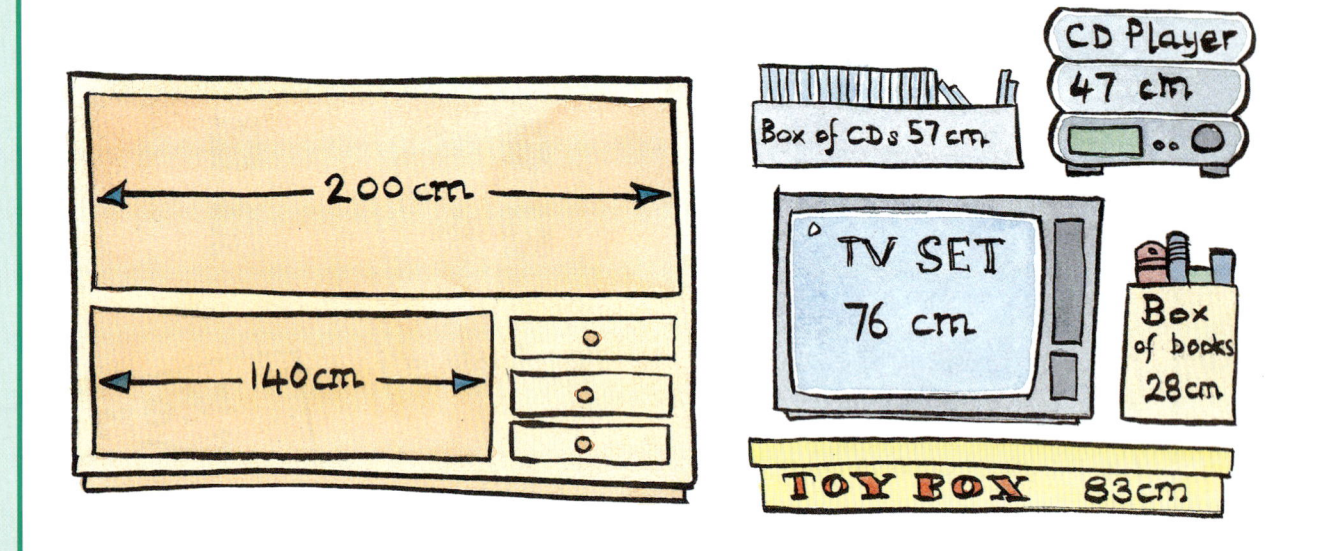

Shelf unit: top shelf 200 cm, bottom shelf 140 cm

Items:
- Box of CDs 57 cm
- CD Player 47 cm
- TV SET 76 cm
- Box of books 28 cm
- TOY BOX 83 cm

a Can she put the TV set and the toy box on the bottom shelf?

b Work out how she can fit all the items on to the shelves.
Show your working.

Check your answers by rounding the measurements to the nearest 10.

C2 Design a diferent shelf unit to take the same items.

| Key idea | We can use doubles of multiples of 10 to check calculations using measures. |

30 AS4 Extending mental strategies: developing a standard written method

AS4.4 Using different strategies to add and subtract

> **Key idea** — We can use all we know about numbers to add and subtract mentally.

Numbers on the diamond grid: 13, 26, 47, 41, 35, 34, 16, 28, 17, 24, 32, 45, 42, 36, 25, 38

A1

a Find 3 pairs of numbers that are near doubles.
Add them together and show your working.

b Now try subtracting the numbers.

B1 Find 3 pairs of numbers with units digits that are less than 6.

Add some of them and subtract some of them.

Use an empty number line to help explain your method.

B2 Find more pairs of numbers to add or subtract.

Record your method.

AS4 Extending mental strategies: developing a standard written method

AS4.5 Choosing ways to add in columns

> **Key idea** — When we use columns to help add HTU we can start with the hundreds or with the units.

A1 Practise using columns to add.

Try some with units first and some with hundreds first.

- goggles £18
- rubber dinghy £115
- wetsuit (small) £66
- surfboard £129
- flippers £25
- divers watch £179
- oars £38
- snorkel £21

You have £200 to spend.
What can you buy?

Remember to line up units under units, tens under tens and hundreds under hundreds

B1
- a 236 + 58
- b 143 + 84
- c 375 + 124
- d 268 + 227
- e 184 + 273
- f 8 + 139 + 46

B2

- Sea fishing trip £359 for 5 days
- Bargains! Rods £126, Camera £236, Watch £179, Wetsuit £134
- Waterskiing lessons £185 for 10 lessons
- boat hire £283 for 1 week

Find the cost of

- a the sea fishing trip and a rod
- b waterskiing lessons and a wetsuit
- c boat hire and a camera
- d a camera and a watch

C1 Fred has £750 to spend.
What can he buy?

AS5.1 Using pattern to add a single digit

Key idea | We can use pattern to add a single digit.

B1 You need CM 16 and a dice.

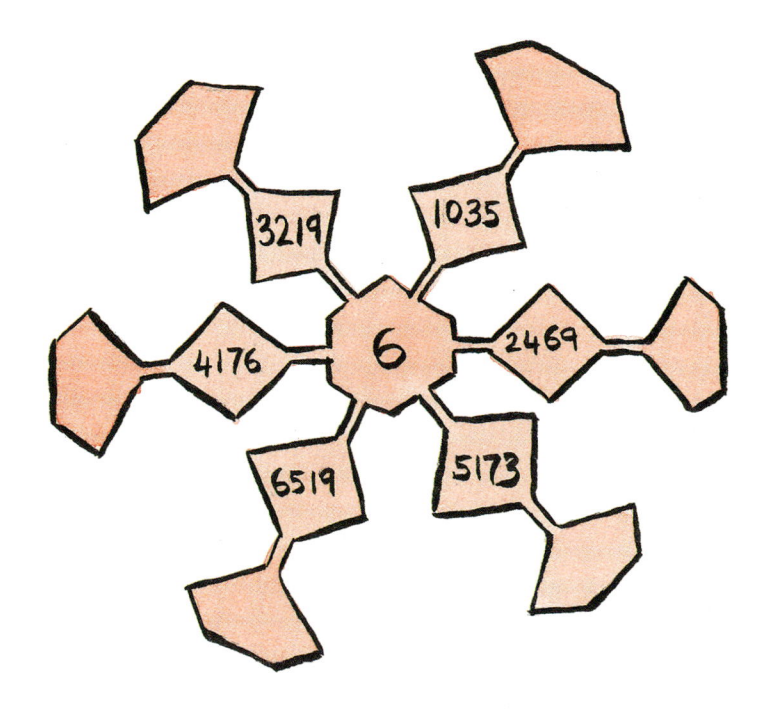

[Snowflake diagram with centre "6" and numbers 3219, 1035, 2469, 5173, 6519, 4176 around it]

- Write 6, 7, 8, 9 in the centre of the snowflakes.

- Throw a dice 4 times to make 4-digit numbers to put in the first ring of circles.

- Add to fill in the outside ring of circles.

C1 What different values can you find to make these true?

a 7259 + ☐ is less than 7262 + 3

b 8517 + ☐ is less than 8521 + 5

C2 Penny is playing 'Two dice'.
She starts at 174 and throws 4 steps of 3.
Where does she land?
What other dice throws would get her to the same place?

AS5 Developing strategies for 3- and 4-digit numbers: mental and informal written methods

AS5.2 Using pattern to subtract a single digit 1

| Key idea | We can subtract a single digit from a multiple of 100 or 1000 by knowing pairs that make 10. |

A1

a Copy this function machine. Fill in the output.

Subtract 6	
Input	Output
500	
700	
900	

b Change the label on the machine to 'Subtract 8'.
Fill in the output for the new machine.

A2 Class 4 went on an outing to the air display.

a Sam had £1. He bought a sweet costing 6p.
How much did he have left?

b Molly had £1. She bought a magazine.
Her change was 6p. How much did she spend?

c Tom's teacher had saved £200. He bought
a radio-controlled plane and had £8 left.
How much did the plane cost?

Remember there are 100p in £1.

B1 **a** Copy this function machine. Fill in the output.

Subtract 4	
Input	Output
4000	
7000	
9000	

b Change the label on the machines to 'Subtract 9'.
Fill in the output for the new machine.

B2 **a** Peter had four 50p coins.
He bought a book and got 7p change.
How much did the book cost?

b Bijur had four £2 coins, two 50p coins and a £1 coin.
He bought a tape and had 9p left.
How much was the tape?

c Joe was 7 in the year 2000. When was he born?

C1 Make up subtraction problems using £10.

Key idea	We can subtract a single digit from a multiple of 100 or 1000 by knowing pairs that make 10.

AS5 Developing strategies for 3- and 4-digit numbers: mental and informal written methods

AS5.3 Using pattern to subtract a single digit 2

> **Key idea** We can use number facts we know to subtract a single digit.

A1 Class 4 went on a school trip to the air display.
Find out how much child had left.

- **a** Sally had £1.81. She gave 7p to her friend Anne.
- **b** Zofia had £2.52. She dropped a 5p coin and could not find it.
- **c** David put 9p in a slot machine. He started with £4.92.

A2 Find out how much each cost.

- **a** Mohammed bought a kite. He had 8p left from £6.75.
- **b** Samantha bought a toy dog. She had 6p left from £5.62.
- **c** The price for the coach was £132. The coach firm took £9 off to help the school pay for it.

B Do CM 18.   *Use number facts to 20.*

C1 Look at your results from B.
Find out when the units digit repeats if you keep decreasing by

- **a** 2
- **b** 5
- **c** 3
- **d** 10

C2
- **a** What other numbers will take 5 steps? Check your answer.
- **b** What other numbers will take 10 steps? Check your answer.
- **c** What other numbers will take 2 steps? Check your answer.

AS5.5 Using addition and subtraction facts

> **Key idea** We can use any addition fact we know, or have found out, to make a set of addition and subtraction sentences.

A1
- **a** 56 + 41 = 97   so   97 − 41 = ☐
- **b** 49 + 32 = 81   so   81 − 49 = ☐
- **c** 96 − 43 = 53   so   43 + 53 = ☐
- **d** 93 − 35 = 58   so   58 + 35 = ☐

B1 Mad Max and Blue Baron have 360 minutes of flying time to share.

There are a lot of answers to the problem ☐ + △ = 360

- **a** Find the answer if ☐ and △ are equal.
- **b** Find an answer with both the numbers even.
- **c** Find an answer with both the numbers odd.
- **d** Find an answer with one of the numbers less than 60.
- **e** Find an answer with one of the numbers a multiple of 3.
- **f** Find the answer with one of the numbers twice as big as the other.

B2 Change + to − in B1 **b** − **f**

AS5 Developing strategies for 3- and 4-digit numbers: mental and informal written methods

C1 Find ☐ and then write all the connected sentences.

a 34 + ☐ = 487

b ☐ + 127 = 569

Make sure you have 4 for each.

c 689 − ☐ = 452

d 981 − ☐ = 399

Key idea We can use any addition fact we know, or have found out, to make a set of addition and subtraction sentences.

AS6.3 Reaching the next hundred

> **Key idea** It is often useful to know how to make a number reach the next hundred.

A1 You need a number box made from CM 21.

- **a** Write down a 2-digit number.
- **b** Find the difference between your number and 100. Record on a number line.
- **c** Do **a** and **b** 7 more times.

A2 Find the change from £1 at the DIY shop.

Record on an empty number line.

Remember £1 = 100p

- **a** 79p
- **b** 63p
- **c** 26p
- **d** 58p

AS6 Subtraction by counting up

B1 In the DIY shop hooks come in boxes of 100.

Every month Mr Soames does a stock check to see how many he has sold.

He always starts the month with full boxes, making up boxes of 100 from left over hooks when he can.

Help him find out how many hooks were sold each month.

Use an empty number line to record.

Month	Boxes of hooks at beginning of month	Hooks left at end of month
January	8	7 boxes and 64
February	7	6 boxes and 48
March	7	6 boxes and 23
April	6	5 boxes and 37
May	5	4 boxes and 67
June	5	4 boxes and 55
July	4	3 boxes and 72
August	4	3 boxes and 81
September	3	2 boxes and 59
October	2	1 box and 84
November	2	1 box and 63
December	1	23

AS6 Subtraction by counting up

B2 How much change from £5?

Record on an empty number line.

a screwdriver £4.49

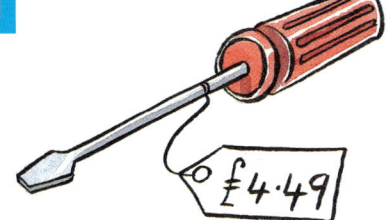

b dustpan and brush £4.36

c 10 tiles £4.19

d bucket £3.85

C1
a 3600 + ☐ = 4000
b 1500 + ☐ = 2000
c 900 + ☐ = 8000
d ☐ + 400 = 10 000

C2 Ask a partner quick questions about making numbers up to the next 100 or 1000.

Key idea It is often useful to know how to make a number reach the next hundred.

AS6 Subtraction by counting up

41

AS6.5 HTU−HTU: Subtraction by counting up

Key idea | Line up decimal points to record money in columns.

★1 Use coins to find change from £5.

a £3.99

b £2.97

c £1.66

A1 Use a 0–1000 number line to help you count up.

a)
```
  3 2 1
− 1 6 9
```
☐ to reach 170
☐☐ to reach 200
☐☐☐ to reach 300
☐☐ to reach 321

b)
```
  6 3 3
− 4 7 6
```
☐ to reach 480
☐☐ to reach 500
☐☐☐ to reach 600
☐☐ to reach 633

A2 Do these in the same way as in A1.

a)
```
  5 4 2
− 3 7 6
```

b)
```
  3 0 6
− 1 7 4
```

A3 Find the difference in price.
Record in columns.

a £3.83    £1.78

b

£4.89   £8.25

Solve these problems.

Give an approximate answer.

Then record in columns.

B1 What is the difference between £378 and £507?

B2 My lunch cost £3.78. I paid with a £5 note.

How much change do I get?

B3 I have saved £1.89 for a football that costs £6.73.

How much more do I need?

B4 I have £12.60 but I owe my mum £8.70.

How much will I have left when I pay her?

C1 My brother got £56.50 for his birthday.

I got £78.20 for mine.

How much more did I get than my brother?

C2 On Monday the tuck shop took £102.20.

On Tuesday it took £97.80.

How much more was taken on Monday than Tuesday?

C3 My ambition is to save £1000. So far I have got £67.80.

How much more must I save?

| Key idea | Line up decimal points to record money in columns. |

AS6 Subtraction by counting up

AS7.1 Starting with the units

Key idea | We can start with the units when recording mental addition in columns.

Rulers: 135, 47

Paint trays: 138, 81

Crayons: 36 (fine crayons), 118 (Crayons), 125 (CHUBBY crayons)

A1   How many rulers altogether?

A2   How many paint trays altogether?

A3   How many crayons altogether?

AS7 Adding with carrying

STOCK LIST

Pencils
- HB 345
- 2H 78

A3 paper
- best 175
- rough 256

Felt pens
- fine 132
- medium 245
- bold 78

Notebooks
- plain 145
- lined 367

Paper clips
- normal 554
- jumbo 678

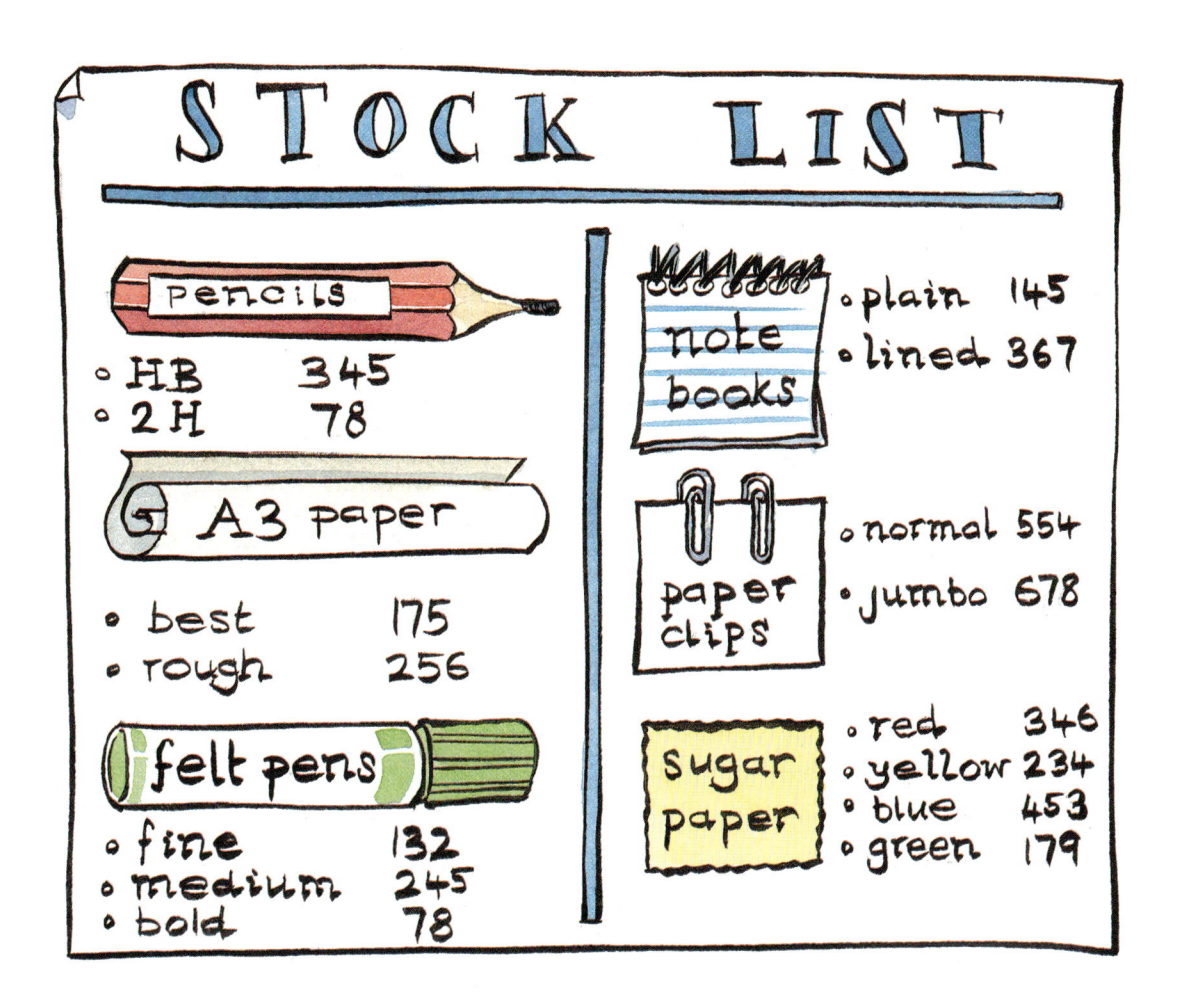

Sugar paper
- red 346
- yellow 234
- blue 453
- green 179

B1 How many pencils altogether?

B2 How many sheets of A3 paper altogether?

B3 How many felt pens altogether?

C1 How many notebooks altogether?

C2 How many paperclips altogether?

C3 How many sheets of sugar paper altogether?

| Key idea | We can start with the units when recording mental addition in columns. |

AS7 Adding with carrying

AS7.2 A short way of recording in columns

> **Key idea** We can use a short way of recording addition in columns.

Work in pairs.

All the children in an after-school club did a sponsored silence and collected money to buy some new games.

Child	Amount
Ali	£3.24
Ben	53p
Catherine	£4.45
Danny	£2.44
Elizabeth	£5.02
Fay	£2.34
George	41p
Harry	£1.30

1 a Put the children in pairs.
Add in columns to find out how much each pair has.

b How many different pairings could there be?

2 a What would be the best pairings for buying games?

b Explain why.

AS7 Adding with carrying

AS7.3 Carrying to other columns

Key idea We can 'carry' an amount to another column when we add in columns.

Work in groups.

Use the short way of recording in columns to work out the problems.

Take care with money sums. Keep pounds under pounds, 10 pence under 10 pence and pence in the pennies column.

1. Isla collects marbles.
   She had 147.
   Then a friend gave her his collection of 139.
   How many has she got now?

2. Jeremy's dad has 263 CDs.
   His uncle has 82 more than his dad.
   How many CDs does his uncle have?

3. Kim and Jayne both collected 1p coins for charity.
   Kim had £6.68.
   Jayne had £5.26.
   How much did they have altogether?

4. Emma gave her horse 245 carrots each month.
   The vet said she should increase the number by 70 carrots each month.
   How many carrots must she give it each month?

5. I spent £4.78 at the post office and £1.05 at the farm shop.
   How much did I spend altogether?

6. In a survey Cassandra and Raj counted 354 cars and 171 lorries going past.
   What was the sum of the cars and lorries?

7. It cost the Adams family £6.35 to go into a theme park and another £3.08 for drinks.
   What was the total cost of their trip?

8. Jamie did 253 hops on his pogo stick.
   His friend Dan did 229.
   How many hops did they do altogether?

AS7 Adding with carrying

AS7.5 Adding several numbers in columns

Key idea: We can add several numbers in columns.

In each question add to find **a** how many altogether
b the total value

B1

Rulers	Number	Total value
wooden	123	£3.24
plastic	231	£5.05
short	45	70p

B2

Pens	Number	Total value
fine	206	£5.28
medium	73	£2.43
bold	115	£2.05

B3

Pencils	Number	Total value
HB	470	£5.45
2H	144	£2.54
crayons	25	£1.30

B4

Sugar paper	Number of sheets	Total value
red	270	£8.10
blue	158	£4.74
green	206	£6.18
yellow	87	£2.61

AS8.2 Adjusting from tens to units to help subtract

> **Key idea** We can adjust from tens to units to help us subtract.

Use the short way of recording to help solve the problems.

A1 John scored 563.
His little brother James scored 35 fewer.
What was James' score?

A2 The longest boot-lace sweet in town was 685 cm.
It decreased by 58 cm when class 4 had a piece each.
How long was it then?

B1 Jade counted 272 days to Christmas.
64 days later, how long was it to Christmas?

B2 There are 365 days in a year.
If you go to school for 207 days,
how many days in a year do you not have school?

You could use a calendar to check.

B3 It takes 753 paces to walk round the playground.
It takes 527 paces to walk around the hall.
What is the difference in the number of paces?

C Work with a partner. Do C1 several times.

C1 Write down a 3-digit number each.

Subtract the smaller from the larger mentally.
Record what you did on a number line.
Now use the short way to subtract if you can.

C2
  a Make a list of the pairs where you need to adjust the units to subtract.

  b Talk about how you could adjust the other pairs to let you subtract.

AS8 Subtraction with decomposition

AS8.4 Subtracting 3-digit numbers

> **Key idea** Line up the decimal points to subtract money in columns.

★1 a) 45p − 22p   b) 66p − 38p   c) 82p − 27p

Use coins to help

★2 a) £2.35 − £1.18   b) £5.92 − £2.46   c) £4.84 − £4.37

A1 Help the controllers to plan their work.

Find the difference between the numbers of planes landing during each shift.

Work in columns.

a) 136 and 89   b) 242 and 128   c) 360 and 145
d) 357 and 182   e) 229 and 173   f) 406 and 284
g) 314 and 189   h) 231 and 85   i) 341 and 268

A2 Choose 4 presents from the airport shop.

Find the difference in price for all the pairs.

Record in columns.

(Airport shop prices: £2.25, £1.25, £6.50, £4.99, £3.75, £0.75)

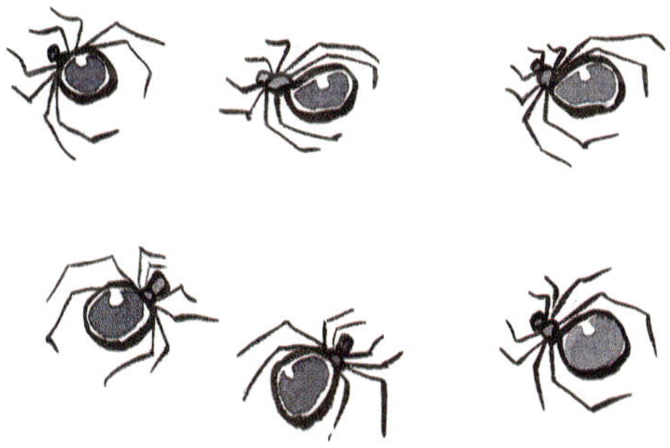

MD1.1 Add and multiply

Key idea	4 + 4 + 4 is the same as 4 × 3

A1 Copy the grids. Add to complete them.

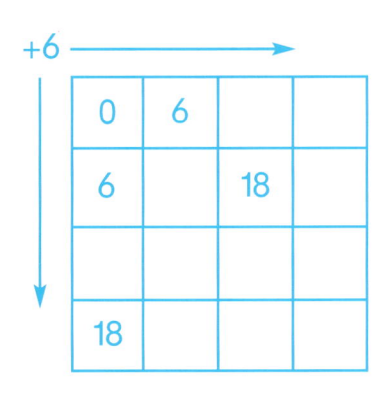

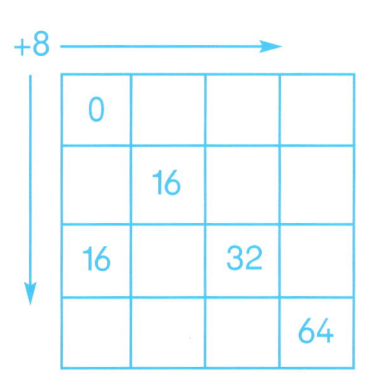

a) +6 →

0	6	
6		18
18		

b) +8 →

0		
	16	
16		32
		64

A2 How many legs?

a) 
2 + 2 + 2 + 2 + 2 + 2 + 2 + 2
= 2 × 8 = ☐

b) 
4 + 4 + 4 + 4 + 4 + 4 + 4
= 4 × 7 = ☐

c) 
6 + 6 + 6 + 6 + 6
= 6 × 5 = ☐

d)
8 + 8 + 8 + 8 + 8 + 8
= 8 × 6 = ☐

MD1 Understanding multiplication and division

51

B1 Copy the grids. Multiply to complete them.

Use repeated addition to find the answers you don't know.

a

×	2	3	4	5
2				
4				
6				
8				

b

×	6	7	8	9
2				
4				
6				
8				

a (bat) b (lizard) c (spider) d (beetle)

C1 For each creature, imagine you can see 48 legs altogether.

Write how many creatures like this.

a 2 × ☐ = 48

C2 Do the same as C1 for 72 legs.

Write down how you worked out each multiplication sentence.

C3 Choose another total and write multiplication sentences for each creature.

Key idea 4 + 4 + 4 is the same as 4 × 3

MD1.3 Multiply and divide

> **Key idea** Multiplying undoes dividing, and dividing undoes multiplying.

A1 Use multiplication facts you know.

a. $3 \times \square = 24$
b. $\square \times 5 = 45$
c. $3 \times 7 = \square$
d. $36 \div 4 = \square$
e. $27 \div 3 = \square$
f. $35 \div 5 = \square$

A2 A young kangaroo has to leap 24 m altogether to catch up with his mother.

He could do 24 very small leaps of 1 m.

Find other ways he could reach her.

Write your answers like this.

$24 \div \square = \square$

B1 **At the safari zoo**

Write down division sentences.

Work out how much each animal has eaten.

a. 4 chimps have eaten 28 bananas altogether.

b. 10 seals have eaten 100 fish altogether.

c. 5 elephants have eaten 40 bales of hay altogether.

B2 Check your answers to B1 by multiplying.

Write a sentence for each one.

MD1 Understanding multiplication and division

B3 Copy and complete these trails.

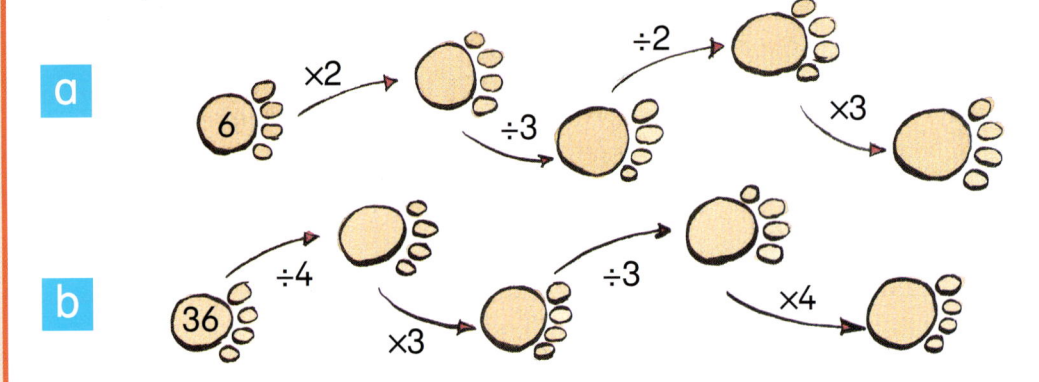

a) 6 →×2→ ☐ →÷3→ ☐ →÷2→ ☐ →×3→ ☐

b) 36 →÷4→ ☐ →×3→ ☐ →÷3→ ☐ →×4→ ☐

C1 Try these number trails.

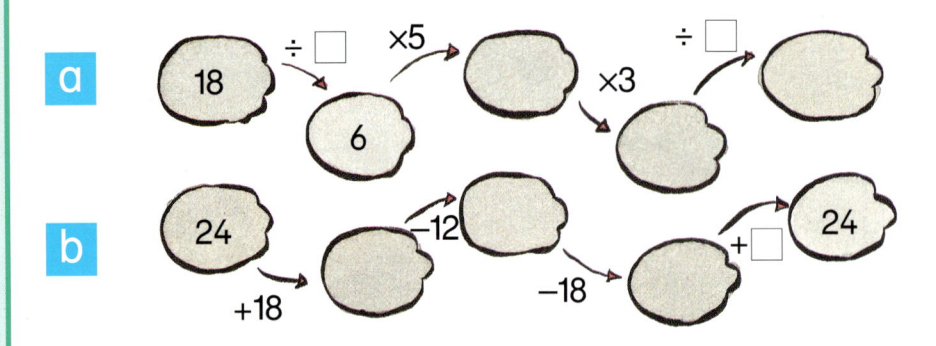

a) 18 →÷☐→ 6 →×5→ ☐ →×3→ ☐ →÷☐→ ☐

b) 24 →+18→ ☐ →−12→ ☐ →−18→ ☐ →+☐→ 24

C2 a) Play 'Think of a number' several times:

Think of a number.
Multiply it by 5.
Add 13.
Take away 8.
Divide it by 5.
Take 1.
Divide by the number you first thought of.
Write down your answer.

b) Try it out on a friend. Tell them what to do, but they must not tell you the answer.

Reveal the answer and amaze them.

Key idea	Multiplying undoes dividing, and dividing undoes multiplying.

MD1 Understanding multiplication and division

MD2.2 Which way round?

Key idea | We can multiply numbers in any order, so if we know 7 × 8 = 56, we also know that 8 × 7 = 56.

★1

3 × 7 = 21

7 × 3 = 21

Write 2 multiplication facts for **a** – **f**

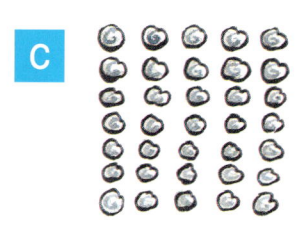

a   b   c

d   e   f

★2 **You need a partner and about 40 cubes to share.**

Make different arrays and record each one.

Use at least 20 cubes each time.

A1 **You need a partner and 48 cubes to share.**

Make different arrays and record each one.

Each time • use at least 30 cubes

• write 2 multiplication facts

B1 **You need a partner and 48 cubes to share.**

Use all the cubes to make different arrays.

Record each one with 2 multiplication facts.

C1 **You need a partner and 96 cubes to share.**

Repeat B1.

MD2 Using known multiplication facts

55

MD2.4 Using multiplication facts 1

Key idea | We can use many strategies to work out multiplication facts we don't know from facts that we do know.

★1
a 4 × 5 = ☐   b 3 × 3 = ☐   c 5 × 6 = ☐
d 7 × 3 = ☐   e 2 × 8 = ☐   f 4 × 4 = ☐

Remember 5 × 6 = 6 × 5
4 × 4 = double 2 × 4

Remember 2 × 6 is double 2 × 3

★2 Sam has made some amazing sandcastles. They each have 6 flags.

How many flags does he need for these numbers of sandcastles?

a 2   b 4   c 6

A1
a 6 × 4 = ☐   b 5 × 8 = ☐   c 3 × 6 = ☐
d 5 × 7 = ☐   e 4 × 9 = ☐   f 6 × 9 = ☐

A2 Spider crabs have 8 legs and 2 claws.

How many claws and how many legs do these numbers of spider crabs have?

Remember 7 × 8 = (8 × 8) − (1 × 8)

a 4   b 8   c 7   d 9

A3 Write down the strategies you used to solve A2.

56   MD2 Using known multiplication facts

B1
a) 6 × 6 = ☐
b) 6 × 8 = ☐
c) 9 × 7 = ☐
d) 8 × 8 = ☐
e) 9 × 9 = ☐
f) 7 × 8 = ☐

B2 There's a beach volley ball competition today.

Each children's team has 4 members.

Each game has 2 teams and an adult referee playing 3 rounds.

Each round lasts 7 minutes.

There are 8 games being played.

a) How many children play?

b) Add in the referees to find out how many people are taking part.

c) How many balls are needed?

d) How many minutes of play are there in each game?

C1
a) ☐ × 7 = 63
b) 8 × ☐ = 64
c) 7 × ☐ = 56
d) ☐ × ☐ = 81
e) ☐ × ☐ = 49
f) 9 × ☐ = 54

C2
a) Write down the letters of the facts you didn't know in C1.

b) Explain the strategy you used to find the answer.

C3 You need IP 5 and a partner.

Make up some problems using multiplication facts for a friend to solve.

Swap problems, solve and give them back to your partner to check.

Key idea We can use many strategies to work out multiplication facts we don't know from facts that we do know.

MD2 Using known multiplication facts

MD3.1 Using multiplication facts 2

Key idea We can use the multiplication fact 4 × 5 = 20 to find 40 × 5.

Penguin 20p, Kangaroo 50p, Chimpanzee 70p, Panda 30p

Lion 60p, Zebra 40p, Elephant 80p, Giraffe 90p

A1 Find the cost of buying these cards.

- a 6 zebra cards
- b 7 penguin cards
- c 8 kangaroo cards
- d 9 panda cards

A2
- a 5 lion cards and 4 giraffe cards
- b 6 chimpanzee cards and 3 elephant cards

B1 Work out the change from £5 after buying these postcards.

- a 8 zebra cards
- b 5 lion cards
- c 3 giraffe cards
- d 7 kangaroo cards
- e 6 panda cards
- f 4 chimpanzee cards

C1 Work out the change from £10 after buying these postcards.

- a 4 giraffe cards and 6 zebra cards
- b 6 panda cards and 4 lion cards
- c 5 kangaroo cards and 5 panda cards
- d 8 lion cards and 6 penguin cards

58 MD3 Using the associative and distributive laws for TU × U

MD3.2 Multiplying with money

> **Key idea** We can split 2-digit numbers to make them easier to multiply.

There are plans to set up a stamp club in school.

Each member will need:

- **a** a stamp album
- **b** tweezers
- **c** a magnifying glass
- **d** stamps starter pack
- **e** a pencil
- **f** a notepad

Stamp Album 32p
24p
36p
Starter pack 28p
17p
Notes 43p

A1 Find how much each of **a** – **f** costs for 3 children.

B1
- **a** How much would it cost to set up the club for 5 children?
- **b** Use this to find the cost for 30 children.

C There is only £36 available to set up the club.

C1 How many children could come?

C2 More children could come if each child paid a small amount.

Investigate how much each child needs to pay if 30 children want to join the club.

MD3 Using the associative and distributive laws for TU × U

MD4.1 Sharing equally

> **Key idea** We can divide a total by sharing equally.

Feeding the animals

Work with a partner.
Choose at least 2 problems from A and 2 problems from B.
Find the quotient each time.
Be ready to share your ways of solving the problems in the plenary.

A1 Share 24 bananas equally between 8 monkeys.

A2 There are 50 carrots to share equally among 10 rabbits.
How many carrots will each rabbit get?

A3 30 fish are to be shared equally among 6 sea-lions.
How many fish will each sea-lion eat?

A4 If 12 lettuces are shared equally among 4 tortoises,
how many lettuces will each tortoise receive?

B1 A farmer wants to give each of his 5 pigs 4 apples.
If he has 22 apples will he have enough to do this?

B2 A zoo keeper shares 20 sticks of bamboo equally among 3 pandas and puts the remaining sticks away. How many sticks does he put away?

B3 36 feeding bowls need to be stacked in piles of 5.
How many piles will there be?

B4 At feeding time 4 guinea pigs eat at each feeding bowl.
If there are 30 guinea pigs, how many bowls are needed?

MD4.2 Rounding

Key idea | Sometimes we need to round 'up' and sometimes 'down' to make sense of a sharing problem.

- Do the calculations.
- Think about the remainders.
- Round up or down to give the answer.
- Write a sentence to explain your rounding.

A1 I can fit 5 sandwiches on a plate.
How many plates will I need for 24 sandwiches?

A2 4 children and a driver can travel in a car.
How many cars will be needed to take 10 children to the airport?

A3 Chewy bars cost 10p each.
How many can I buy for 35p?

A4 Tennis balls are packed in tubes of 3.
How many tubes can be made from 43 balls?

A5 5 fish can be kept in a tank. How many tanks are needed for 88 fish?

You could think about 10 fish in a tank first.

B1 Make up division stories to match the division sentences.
Explain whether you need to round the answer up or down.

a) $34 ÷ 5 = 6 \text{ r } 4$ b) $69 ÷ 12 = 5 \text{ r } 9$ c) $184 ÷ 50 = 3 \text{ r } 34$

- Do the calculations.
- Think about the remainders.
- Round up or down to give the answer.
- Write a sentence to explain your rounding.

C1 I can fit 7 cups on a tray.
How many trays will I need for 54 cups?

C2 A minibus can transport 12 children.
How many minibuses will be needed to transport 75 children?

C3 Cookies cost 9p each.
How many can I buy for £1.00?

C4 6 plants can be planted in each tub.
How many tubs are needed for 58 plants?

C5 There are 8 flowers in each bunch.
How many bunches can be made from 60 flowers?

C6 Choose your own division sentences.
Make up problems to swap with your partner.

Key idea Sometimes we need to round 'up' and sometimes 'down' to make sense of a sharing problem.

MD4.4 Dividing bigger numbers

> **Key idea** We need to record working for division of bigger numbers.

C1 Work with a partner.

Choose one of the questions below to solve in your own way.
Record your method and explain why you used it underneath.

- **a** Sweets are packed in bags of 8.
  How many bags can be made from 150 sweets?

- **b** A plate holds 7 cakes.
  How many plates will be needed to hold 95 cakes?

- **c** 9 children can sit at a table.
  How many tables are needed for 200 children?

- **d** The River Rapids ride at the theme park takes 6 passengers in each canoe. How many canoes are needed for 84 passengers?

- **e** Rabbits eat 7 carrots each day.
  How many rabbits can be fed with 120 carrots?

- **f** Tickets to a play cost £8. How many tickets can be bought with £130?

- **g** Chairs are stacked in piles of 6. How many piles will 112 chairs make?

- **h** Books are displayed 9 to a shelf.
  How many shelves will display 160 books?

C2 Now choose another question and solve it.

Record your method and explain it clearly underneath.

MD4 Developing informal written methods for TU ÷ U

MD5.1 Multiplying by 10 or 100

> **Key idea** Multiplying by 10 moves digits 1 place to the left.
> Multiplying by 100 moves digits 2 places to the left.

A1
a 12 × 10 = ☐   b 23 × 10 = ☐   c 35 × 10 = ☐
d 5 × 100 = ☐   e 14 × 100 = ☐   f 70 × 10 = ☐

A2 Work with a partner.

a There are 10 stickers in a pack.
How many stickers in 15 packs?
Write a number sentence.

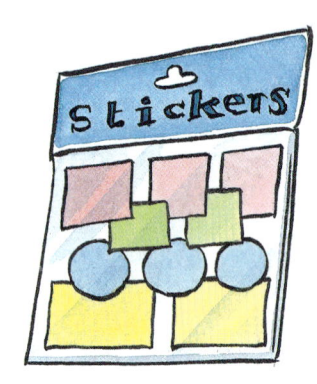

b Put 10 biscuits on each plate.
How many biscuits for 25 plates?

A3 Make up two '×100' problems for your partner to solve.

B1
a 272 × 10 = ☐   b 384 × 10 = ☐   c 740 × 10 = ☐

B2
a 16 × ☐ = 160   b 51 × ☐ = 510   c ☐ × 75 = 750

B3
a 23 × 100 = ☐   b 48 × 100 = ☐   c 40 × 100 = ☐
d 98 × 100 = ☐   e ☐ × 100 = 1500   f 100 × ☐ = 1000

MD5 Working towards short multiplication for TU × U

B4 Work with a partner.

Write a number sentence to solve each problem.

a There are 10 packets of crisps in a multipack.
How many in 150 multipacks?

b 100 children each have 25p.
How much money altogether?

c 1250 wiggling toes.
How many children?

C1 Make up story problems for your partner to solve.

Use ×10 and ×100 with 3-digit numbers.

| Key idea | Multiplying by 10 moves digits 1 place to the left. Multiplying by 100 moves digits 2 places to the left. |

MD5 Working towards short multiplication for TU × U

MD5.2 Multiplying by 'near 10' numbers

Key idea | To multiply by a 'near 10' number, multiply by 10 and adjust.

Rope Street Primary School has 7 classes.

Ravi wants to work out how much it costs to buy a pencil for each child.

Here is the class list.

R	Y1	Y2	Y3	Y4	Y5	Y6
29	30	27	31	28	32	26

Pencils cost 9p each.

Write down how you work out the answer each time.

A1 How much do pencils cost for each class?

A2 How many pencils are needed for the whole school?

    a Estimate   **b** Calculate

A3 How much does it cost to buy pencils for the whole school?

Rope street primary School Shop

- Nuts & Raisins — 9p / 11p
- Banana — 9p
- Tomato ketchup — 9p
- Orange — 9p
- Chocolate bar — 10p / 11p
- Apple — 10p / 11p
- Cheesy snacks — 10p
- Cream cheese — 9p
- Grapes — 11p

You need some number cards from a 1–100 set.

B1 For each item in the shop:

- **a** Choose a number card to tell how many have been sold.
- **b** Calculate how much money the shop has taken.

C1 Choose some 3-digit numbers to multiply by 9 or 11.

Multiply by 10 and adjust if you need to.

Key idea | To multiply by a 'near 10' number, multiply by 10 and adjust.

MD5 Working towards short multiplication for TU × U

MD6.1 Multiplying quickly

| Key idea | We can start from facts we know and double to multiply some numbers. |

Do these as fast as you can.

A1
- a 3 × ☐ = 21
- b ☐ × 5 = 20
- c 4 × ☐ = 16
- d ☐ × 3 = 27
- e 5 × ☐ = 30
- f ☐ × 4 = 24

A2
- a 4 × ☐ = 40
- b ☐ × 6 = 48
- c 8 × ☐ = 32
- d ☐ × 9 = 45
- e 7 × ☐ = 63
- f ☐ × ☐ = 56

A3 ☐ × ☐ = 30

How many different sentences can you make?

B1
- a 3 × ☐ = 210
- b ☐ × 5 = 200
- c 4 × ☐ = 160
- d ☐ × 5 = 300
- e 8 × ☐ = 400
- f ☐ × 3 = 270

B2
- a ☐ × 10 = 600
- b 6 × ☐ = 360
- c 8 × ☐ = 320
- d ☐ × 7 = 280
- e ☐ × 9 = 720
- f ☐ × ☐ = 560

B3 ☐ × ☐ = 240

How many different sentences can you make?

MD6.2 Using columns for TU × U

Key idea We can write down a multiplication using columns for tens and units (short multiplication).

Work these out like this:

21 × 3

```
    2 1
  ×   5
  ─────
  1 0 0     20 × 5
      5     1 × 5
  ─────
  1 0 5
```

Check using a grid:

```
  ×  | 20 | 1
  5  |100 | 5     100 + 5 = 105
```

A1 a 32 × 4   b 31 × 4

A2 a 23 × 3   b 22 × 3

A3 a 41 × 4   b 42 × 4

A4 a 51 × 5   b 61 × 5

Work these out using columns.
Check using a grid.

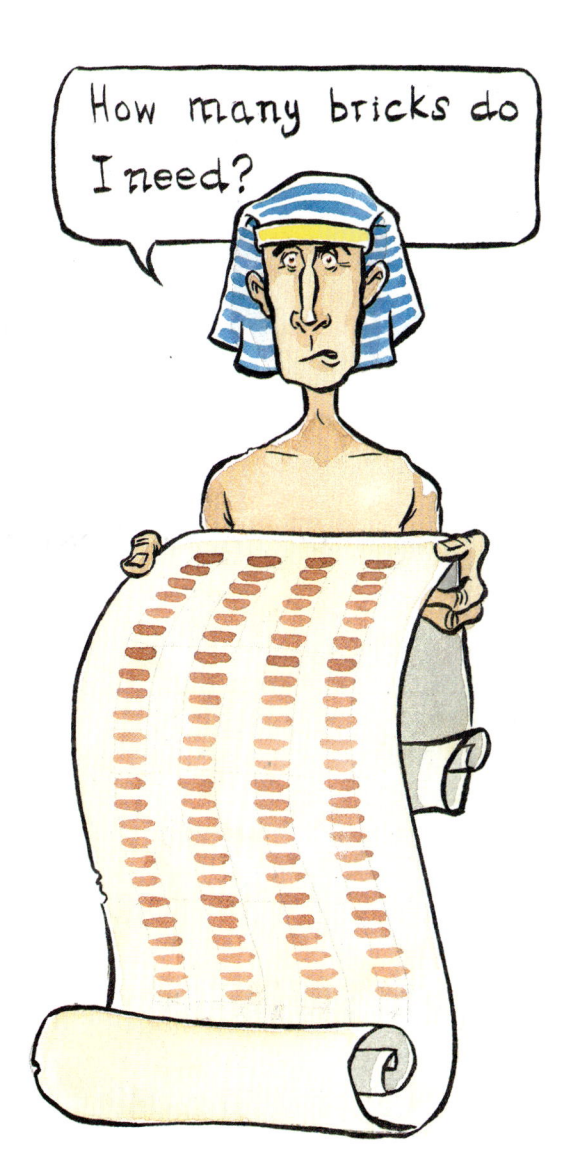

B1 a 33 × 4   b 36 × 4

B2 a 43 × 5   b 45 × 5

B3 a 42 × 6   b 44 × 6

B4 a 53 × 8   b 55 × 8

How many bricks do I need?

MD6 More ways to multiply TU × U: short multiplication

The Ancient Egyptians had a good way to multiply.
They used doubling like this.

31 × 4   31 × 2 = 62

               62 × 2 = 124

         So   31 × 4 = 124   It's easy for ×4!

31 × 6   31 × 2 = 62

               62 × 2 = 124

         So   31 × 6 = 124 + 62
                      = 186

Multiply these numbers the Egyptian way.

C1 Multiply by 4: 21, 26, 32, 43, 55

C2 Multiply 6: 22, 31, 43, 52, 64

C3 How do you think the Egyptians multiplied by 7?

Try some numbers.

| Key idea | We can write down a multiplication using columns for tens and units (short multiplication). |

MD6.3 TU x U: tens first

Key idea We can multiply any 2-digit number using a column method.

Example
```
   2 3
 ×   4
 ─────
   8 0
   1 2
 ─────
   9 2
```

A1 Copy and complete.

a) 44 × 4   b) 54 × 4   c) 64 × 4

d) 35 × 4   e) 36 × 4   f) 37 × 4

A2 Check each answer by doubling and doubling again.

B1 Copy and complete.

a) 55 × 3   b) 63 × 5   c) 68 × 3

d) 74 × 5   e) 76 × 6   f) 83 × 5

B2 Use another way of multiplying to check each answer.

MD6 More ways to multiply TU × U: short multiplication

MD6.4 TU x U: units first

Key idea | We can start with the tens or the units when we record TU x U

MD6.5 TU × U: short multiplication

Key idea | Short multiplication is sometimes useful and quick.

Prices shown:
- Lollipops 7p each
- Toffee 3 for 12p
- Truffles 4 for 52p
- Chocolate bars 34p each
- Sugar mice 16p each
- Fudge sticks 18p each

Work in pairs. Use short multiplication to do these.

B1 Ellie is buying lollipops for her class.

There are 27 children. How much will she pay?

B2 How many sticks of fudge can Ellie buy for £1.00?

B3 Jake buys 9 sugar mice.

How much change does he get from £1.50?

B4 Jake would like to buy 6 chocolate bars.

He has £2.00. Can he afford them?

Explain your answer.

B5 Ellie has £5.00. What can she buy for this?

Work out some of her choices.

MD6 More ways to multiply TU × U: short multiplication

73

MD7.2 Dividing 2-digit numbers

> **Key idea** There are lots of ways we can work out the answer to a division problem.

You need a dice. Play the game 'Exact answers' in a group of 3 or 4:

Each player writes down a number between 50 and 100, e.g Jane writes 62, Zarif writes 75.

Then throw the dice. Everyone divides their chosen number by the score.

You get a point if the dice score divides your number exactly.

So if the score is 3, Zarif works out 75 ÷ 3 = 25, and gets a point.

Jane works out 62 ÷ 3 = 20 r 2, and does not get a point.

The first person to get four points wins.

Check their answers!

★1
- **a** Share 40 cards between 5 people.
- **b** Divide 44 by 4.
- **c** How many groups of 3 can be made from 24?
- **d** 30 divided by 10.
- **e** Is 32 divisible by 5?
- **f** Is 4 a factor of 36?

A1

a Share 85 marbles between 5 people.

b Divide 88 by 4.

c How many groups of 3 can be made from 66?

d 90 divided by 9.

e Is 92 divisible by 5?

f Is 6 a factor of 96?

B1

a Share 78 pencils between 6 people.

b 86 divided by 8.

c How many groups of 5 can be made from 42?

d Is 7 a factor of 84?

e Is 98 divisible by 8?

f Divide 97 by 5.

C1 Stephen, Emily, Arash and Ruhksana try some different dice in 'Exact answers'.

a Dice marked 2, 2, 3, 4, 5, 6.

What number can Stephen write down to be sure of winning?

b Dice marked 2, 3, 4, 5, 6, 8.

What is the best number for Arash to write down?

c Dice marked 2, 3, 4, 5, 6, 8.

Can you find a number that will never score a point?

Key idea | There are lots of ways we can work out the answer to a division problem.

MD7.3 Using columns to record TU ÷ U

Key idea: We can record divisions of TU clearly by using columns.

★1 Copy these. Fill in the missing numbers.

a 42 ÷ 3

```
   4 2
-  □ □     10 × 3
   ———
   1 2
-  □ □     4 × 3
   ———
     0
```

42 ÷ 3 = 10 + 4 = □

b 56 ÷ 4

```
   5 6
-  4 0     10 × □
   ———
   □ □
-  □ □     4 × 4
   ———
     0
```

56 ÷ 4 = □ + □ = □

★2 The keeper has 62 fish for 4 penguins.
Record a division in columns.

a How many fish for each penguin?

a How many are left over?

A1 Work out these divisions to find the secret message.
Record in columns.

a E 56 ÷ 4 =   **b** I 45 ÷ 3 =

c S 85 ÷ 5 =   **d** H 78 ÷ 6 =

e T 92 ÷ 4 =   **f** V 81 ÷ 3 =

g Z 96 ÷ 6 =   **h** O 76 ÷ 4 =

Here's the message:

27 / 15 / 17 / 15 / 23   23 / 13 / 14   16 / 19 / 19

MD7 Towards a standard form for TU ÷ U

Record divisions in columns to solve these.
Some have remainders.

B1 a 78 ÷ 6   b 98 ÷ 8   c 89 ÷ 7

B2 Classes 3, 4 and 5 are off to the safari zoo.

There are 83 children and 12 adults.

a They sit on seats for 4 at lunchtime.
How many seats do they need?

b The zoo gives the children information packs to share in groups of 3.
How many packs do they get?

c The monkeys live in groups of 6.
There are 93 altogether.
How many groups are there?

C1 Find all the numbers between 50 and 100 that could go in the box.

Write them in order with the smallest first.

What patterns can you see?

a ☐ ÷ 4 has a remainder of 1

b ☐ ÷ 5 has a remainder of 2

C2 List the numbers that are in the answers to both C1 a and b.

What patterns can you see? Why do they happen?

C3 Do C1 and C2 again.

a ☐ ÷ 3 has a remainder of 1

b ☐ ÷ 6 has a remainder of 2

C4 Investigate your own pair. What happens if you try bigger remainders?

Key idea We can record divisions of TU clearly by using columns.

MD7 Towards a standard form for TU ÷ U

MD7.4 Introducing short division

> **Key idea** We can use ⟌ when we record division.

★1 Use ⟌ to do these.

a) 27 ÷ 3 = ☐   b) 28 ÷ 4 = ☐   c) 35 ÷ 5 = ☐

★2 Copy these. Fill in the missing numbers.

a) 42 ÷ 3

```
      □ □
   3 ) 4 2
   – 3 0    10 × 3
     ___
     1 2
   – 1 2    □ × 3
     ___
       0
```

b) 56 ÷ 4

```
      □ □
   4 ) 5 6
   – 4 0    10 × □
     ___
     1 6
   – □ □    □ × 4
     ___
       0
```

A1 There are 60 children coming to the party at the zoo.

Each child has

a) a lollipop   b) a pencil   c) a balloon

How many packs for a, b and c?

Use ⟌ to record your answers.

MD7 Towards a standard form for TU ÷ U

A2 On another day the zoo has a party for 95 children. Do A1 again for this party.

A3 Write a division story for a friend to solve using ⟌ .

Use ⟌ to do these.

B1
- a 96 ÷ 8 = ☐
- b 84 ÷ 6 = ☐
- c 98 ÷ 7 = ☐

B2
- a 76 ÷ 6 = ☐
- b 93 ÷ 7 = ☐
- c 94 ÷ 8 = ☐

C1 Tommy worked out some divisions.
He only wrote down the answers.
Mark his work. Put right the answers he got wrong.
Show how you worked them out.

Use any way to record.

- a How many groups of 5 are there in 95? **19**
- b Divide 79 by 3. **25 r 1**
- c Is 4 a factor of 86? **Yes**
- d Is 90 divisible by 6? **Yes**
- e Share 94p between 6 people. **15 r 3**
- f Is 8 a factor of 96? **Yes**
- g 93 ÷ 3 = **21**
- h How many 7-seater taxis are needed for 93 people? **13**

C2 Make up some divisions for a friend to check.

Include some wrong answers!

Try using HTU ÷ U

Key idea We can use ⟌ when we record division.

MD7 Towards a standard form for TU ÷ U

79

SP1.2 Patterns and rules

Key idea | We can explain a pattern or rule in words.

A1 Find the next 3 numbers in each sequence.

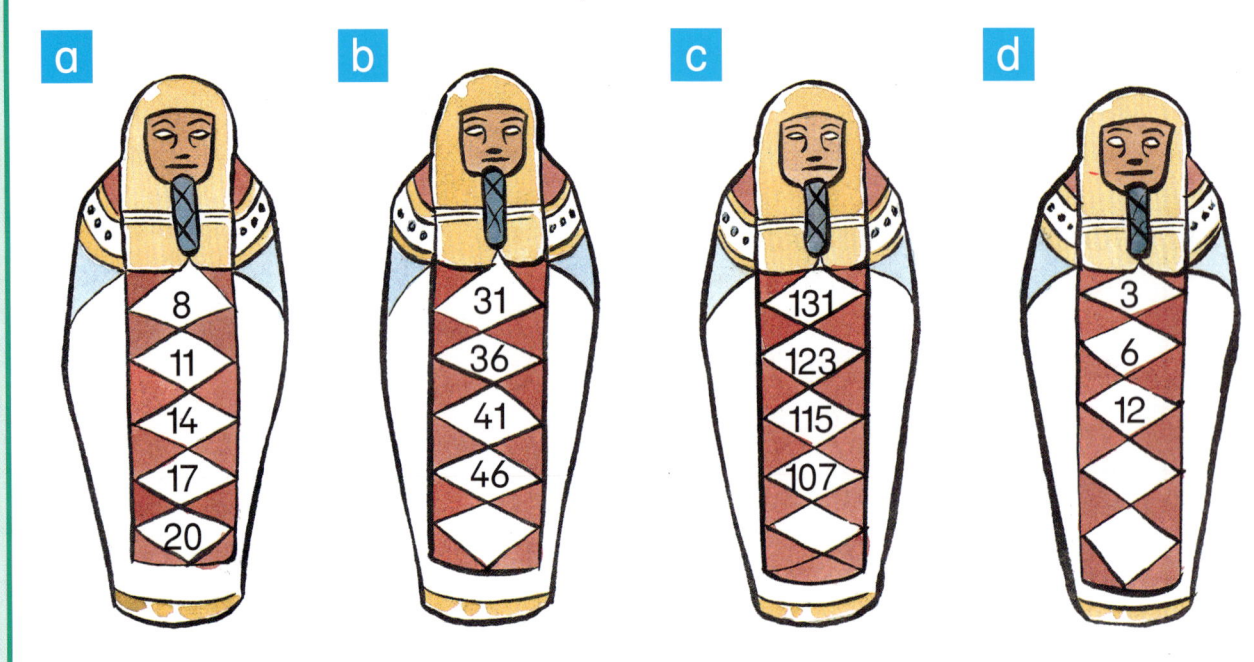

a) 8, 11, 14, 17, 20

b) 31, 36, 41, 46

c) 131, 123, 115, 107

d) 3, 6, 12

A2 Write a rule for each sequence in A1.

Don't forget the starting number.

B1 Find the first 6 numbers in each sequence.

a) Start at 4, Add 6

b) Start at 100, Subtract 8

c) Start at 8000, Halve

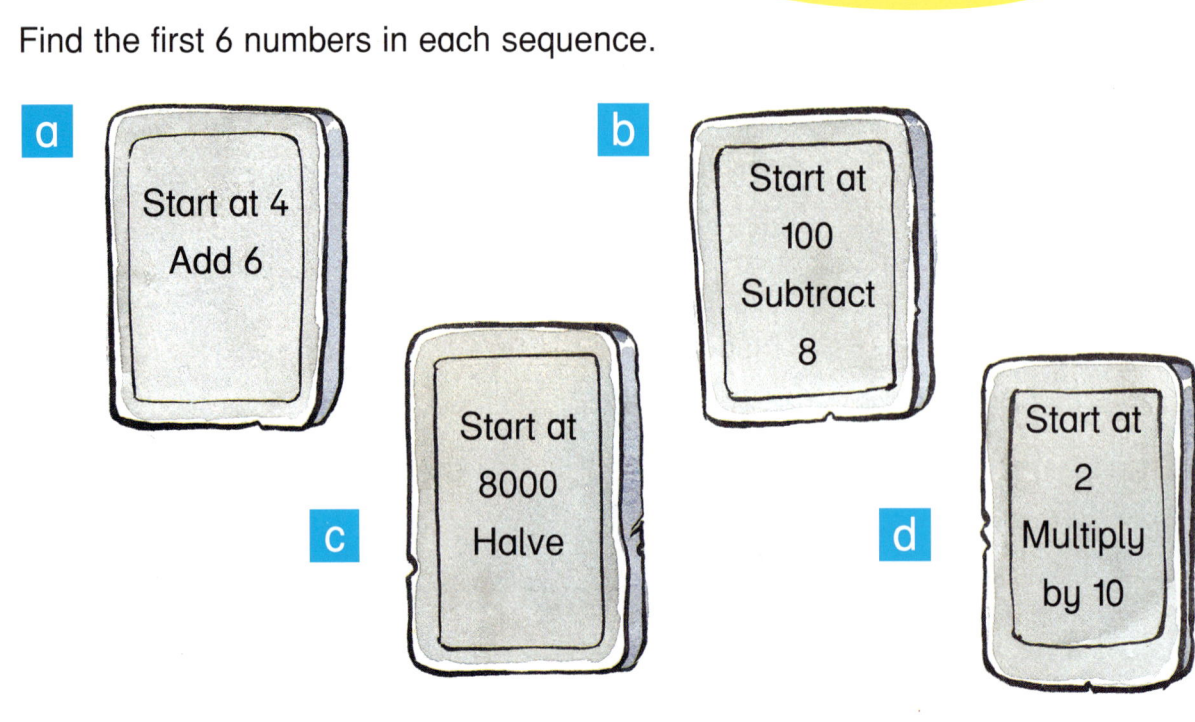

d) Start at 2, Multiply by 10

B2 Write 4 rules to make your own sequences.

B3 You need CM 58.

• Put a blue mark in all the 'multiples of 3' squares.

• Put a yellow mark in all the 'multiples of 4' squares.

Find 3 examples to match each statement.
(They don't have to be numbers on the 1–100 square).

a Multiples of 4 end in 0, 2, 4, 6, or 8.

b Multiples of 3 that are also multiples of 4, are also multiples of 12.

C1 Choose some more multiples to investigate.

Record your finding clearly.

Make a general statement.

C2 Investigate odd and even numbers in multiplication tables.

Record your findings clearly.

Make a general statement.

| Key idea | We can explain a pattern or rule in words. |

SP1.3 Finding solutions

> **Key idea** Sometimes there is more than one solution to a puzzle or problem.

A1 Find the missing numbers.
Check your answers.

a $6 \times \square = 48$

b $20 \div 4 = \square$

c $\square + 26 = 56$

d $101 - \square = 96$

e $\square \times 10 = 90$

f $\square \div 8 = 7$

A2 a Find each of the numbers 1–9 in the magnifying glasses. Each side of the square must add up to 12.

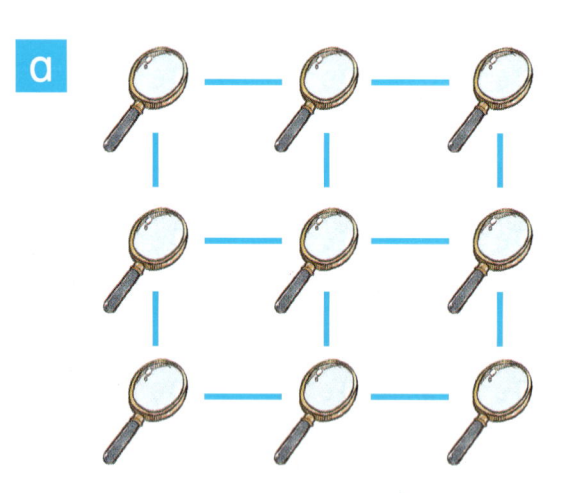

b Copy the grid.
Find the missing numbers.

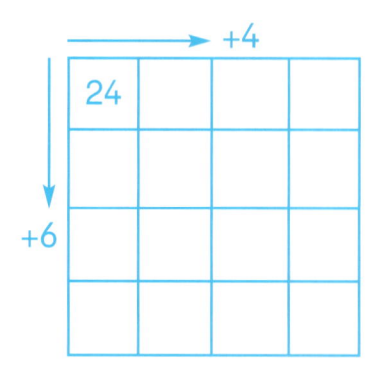

(grid with 24 in top-left cell, +4 across arrow, +6 down arrow)

A3 Choose 2 number sentences from A1.
Make up a mystery in words for Inspector Bloodhound to solve.

82 SP1 Solving problems 1

B1 Inspector Bloodhound is trying to solve the mystery of the missing operations.

One of the numbers is wrong!

Help him complete the grid correctly.

8	13	18	23	
	14		24	
10				
		21		
				33

B2 Find the missing digits.

a 3☐ + △3 = 85   b 8☐ − △9 = 62   c 4☐ + △8 = 110

B3 Inspector Bloodhound investigates 'the park mysteries'.

Write and solve a number sentence for each one.

a 160 rose bushes have gone missing.
He discovers 24 behind the shed.
How many more are still to be found?

b There are 26 wellington boots in the shed.
How many gardeners work in the park?

c One gardener has disappeared.
He was planting 36 pansies in a rectangular pattern.
Find all the ways to finish it.

C1 Find different ways of completing.
Use +, −, × and ÷

a ☐ ○ △ = 125

b ☐ ○ △ = 96

C2 Make up mysteries in words for some of your solutions to C1.

Key idea	Sometimes there is more than one solution to a puzzle or problem.

SP1 Solving problems 1

SP1.4 Explaining word problems

Key idea | Explaining a word problem helps us to solve it.

SP2.2 Explaining how to ...

| Key idea | Describing a rule or pattern helps us to understand how calculations work. |

★1 Add these consecutive numbers.
Write a number sentence.

- a 7, 8
- b 12, 13
- c 24, 25
- d 18, 19
- e 26, 27
- f 32, 33

A1 Hamish says

If you add a pair of consecutive numbers, the total is an odd number.

Give 6 examples to match what Hamish says. Use 1-, 2- and 3-digit numbers.

A2 Talk to your partner about how you added your examples.

Make up a good description of your rule for the Plenary.

SP2 Solving problems 2

85

B1 **a** Investigate adding 3 consecutive numbers.

Begin at 0 and carry on to 20.

Record like this.   0 + 1 + 2 = 3
1 + 2 + 3 =

b Describe the rule for the sequence you make.

B2 Do the same for 4 consecutive numbers to 30.

C1 **a** Investigate adding consecutive numbers.
Try to make all the numbers to 50.

b Describe what you find in a general statement.

Use the patterns you found in B.

Key idea | Describing a rule or pattern helps us to understand how calculations work.

SP3.1 Using + and − to solve problems

Key idea | We can add and subtract using columns when we solve word problems.

Use the short way to add and subtract in columns.

A1

Flights arriving at 10.00

Flight	Passengers	Flight	Passengers
A	261	C	238
B	317	D	105

2 planes are landing at the same time.

Mr Patel is not sure which ones from the 'Flights arriving' board.

Help him find out how many passengers may be arriving at once.

A2 Which flight costs more? Find the difference.

a Majorca or Spain

b Tenerife or Spain

c Majorca or Egypt

d Egypt or Tenerife

Last minute offers

Majorca £149
Spain £125
Tenerife £238
Egypt £357

SP3 Solving problems 3

Here are some distances between cities in Europe.

AIR MILES

London ↔ Amsterdam		217
London ↔ Paris		220
Paris ↔ Amsterdam		261
Paris ↔ Rome		688
London ↔ Rome		898
Rome ↔ Amsterdam		809

B1 Sometimes flights are full.

Then you can take 2 flights, stopping at another place as well.

Find the distances for these 2-stage flights.

a London – Amsterdam – Paris

b London – Paris – Rome

c Paris – Amsterdam – Rome

B2 Find the difference between the distances in B1 and the direct flights.

a London – Paris   b London – Rome   c Paris – Rome

C1 Mrs Smith has 2000 free air miles.

a Find all the ways she could use them.

b How many miles would she have left?

Key idea We can add and subtract using columns when we solve word problems.

SP3 Solving problems 3

SP3.2 Choosing which way to add or subtract

> **Key idea** Sometimes we can easily solve an addition or subtraction problem mentally but sometimes it is better to use a quick column method.

Ali and Liz are trying to win a card game.

Find a total or a difference to help them win.

WINNING ANSWERS
all digits the same!
22, 999, 333, 44, 6666...

You need a partner
0–9 digit cards

A1 Make 2 numbers.
For each, shuffle the cards and take the number you need from the top.

- **a** both 2-digit
- **b** one 2-digit and one 3-digit
- **c** both 3-digit

Add or subtract to see if you have a winning total.

Choose the best way to calculate.
Record each calculation.
Repeat 4 times.

B1 Do A1 again, this time making 3 numbers to add.

- **a** all 2-digit
- **b** two 2-digit and one 3-digit
- **c** all 3-digit
- **d** one 4-digit and two 1-digit

C1 Did you make a winning number in B1?
Investigate.
This time choose a winning number, for example: 666

- **a** Make the first two 2-digit numbers with digit cards.
Find a third number to make sure you win.
- **b** Choose more winning numbers.
Try 2- and 4-digit numbers.

> Think about the size of the 3 numbers.

SP3 Solving problems 3

SP3.3 Using × and ÷ to solve problems

Key idea | Sometimes it is useful to use short multiplication and division to solve problems.

A1 Solve the missing number sentences.

Use short multiplication or division if it helps you.

a 24 × 3 = ☐
b 35 × 6 = ☐
c 21 × ☐ = 84
d 64 ÷ 2 = ☐
e 96 ÷ 6 = ☐
f 90 ÷ ☐ = 30

A2 Find out what you need to make 5 masks.

Each mask needs

a 21 feathers
b 34 sequins
c 12 cm of elastic

B1 Solve the missing number sentences.

Use short multiplication or division if it helps you.

a 48 × 6 = ☐
b 34 × 7 = ☐
c 18 × ☐ = 72
d 125 ÷ ☐ = 25
e 232 ÷ 8 = ☐
f 168 ÷ 7 = ☐

B2 Find out what you need to make 23 leopard masks.
Each mask needs

a 6 pipecleaners
b 9 leopard's spots
c 8 cm of elastic

SP3 Solving problems 3

B3 Use any of these materials to design your own mask.

Sequins 96
Pipe Cleaners 84
Feathers 77
Stars 93
Buttons 79

How many copies of your own mask could you make?

C1 There are 190 tubes in class 4's modelling box.

Class 3 wants at least 40 of them.

Class 4 needs 6 each for their play.

There are 28 children in class 4.

Are there enough tubes for class 3?

Record and explain your working carefully.

C2 Make up a similar problem for a friend to solve.

| Key idea | Sometimes it is useful to use short multiplication and division to solve problems. |

SP3 Solving problems 3

SP3.5 Solving multi-step problems

Key idea | Find an approximate answer before solving a problem; check the answer afterwards.

Monster mash

92 SP3 Solving problems 3